LOS FANTASMAS DE LA FIEBRE

Primera edición: octubre de 2023

ISBN: 978-84-09-54135-5
Depósito Legal: M-008644/2022

www.magarciaguerra.com
magarciaguerra@gmail.com
Instagram: @miguelowar

LOS FANTASMAS DE LA FIEBRE

Miguel Ángel García Guerra

Prólogo

DIME CÓMO CIERRO LAS GRIETAS DE MIS LÁGRIMAS

¿Por qué otro libro sobre el dolor, otro libro sobre la desolación? Porque somos humanos y sufrimos, y es necesario que el sufrimiento que sentimos, siempre individual, sea compartido; porque la virtud de la poesía es esa, expresar pensamientos y sentimientos para comprobar que son compartidos, en definitiva, que no estamos solos.

También porque necesitamos actualizar ese dolor, hacerlo contemporáneo a lo que vivimos en nuestro día a día; de ahí la magia de la literatura, que se renueva constantemente aunque siempre habla de lo mismo: de nosotros.

Y esto es LOS FANTASMAS DE LA FIEBRE, un libro sobre el reencuentro con uno mismo, sobre la reconstrucción personal tras una experiencia personal con todos sus fantasmas que García Guerra nos pone delante a los lectores; un espejo crudo y sincero, pero que, además de servir para comprobar las mermas que el dolor ha hecho en nuestro rostro (y digo rostro como quien dice alma o dice carne o dice sangre), sirve para confirmar que, pese a todo, existimos, y podemos por eso salir de este dolor.

Los fantasmas de la fiebre es un poemario sincero, de esos en los que vemos las vísceras de la hecatombe y, si seguimos en la lectura, la cura de la salvación; un poemario que nos narra un proceso que comienza con una persona vacía 'sin ti', como leemos en el primer poema 'En mi cabeza' hasta una confirmación de la libertad y la fortaleza individual, un soy yo, que leemos en el poema final 'Victoria'.

Porque García Guerra nos propone un camino que recorrer, un camino lleno de miradas y sinceridad con tres estaciones que avanzan y nos hacen entender ese descenso y esa ascensión.

Comenzamos el libro con una primera parte que lleva como entrada 'Me olvidé de mí…'; aquí vemos al poeta perplejo, solo, abandonado. Son poemas donde el dolor de la pérdida de la pareja y la vida que implicaba se hacen explícitos y oscuros 'Zarpazos de desprecio/ desgarran el alma/ con uñas de ira', pero donde siempre (y creo que ese es el ancla que luego servirá para tirar de ella para seguir navegando), hay concesiones a la esperanza y, sobre todo, concesiones al cuidado, a los demás; los hijos miran y no entienden, pero el poeta sí los cuida '¿Cómo serán tus noches,/ cuando yo, insomne, te observe'; por eso no hay absoluta desolación, porque no hay egoísmo.

Más adelante encontramos 'Volver a respirar', el apartado donde hay encuentros, reencuentros, una vida a la que aferrarse más allá del dolor. Una vida a veces apacible y otras furiosa, una vida que conduce al disfrute 'defender que estamos juntos/ riendo desde las alambradas', pero también a la reflexión 'La consciencia de una vida plena', una salida de ese 'pozo' en el que el poeta nos recuerda de vez en cuando que sigue estando, aunque cada vez es 'el pozo más ancho,/ más fácil de escalar, menos oscuro'.

Hay otros, otras a su alrededor; también luz y mar, una apertura a la esperanza, a lo desconocido que trae el presente: acudo a tu encuentro. 'No sé muy bien quién soy/ e ignoro la forma en la que me recibirás en la playa'.

De ahí a 'La calma de la nueva vida', que es un seguir viviendo, mirando el exterior y mirándose a uno mismo que conduce a un reconocimiento de que la fiebre y sus fantasmas están, siguen estando, pero quedan ahí, en estos versos-espejo; porque la literatura es la magia que nos cura y 'Los magos hacen magia y por eso/ no pueden morir'.

José Manuel Gallardo

Agradecimientos

Que esté aquí ahora escribiendo estas palabras de eterna e infinita gratitud no habría sido posible sin el incondicional apoyo de mis hijos, mi familia y de todos los que han estado siempre conmigo, bien en los buenos momentos, bien cuando arreciaba la tormenta.

Gracias, de corazón.

Poemas,
cristales eternos
de emociones esenciales

Me olvidé de mí...

En mi cabeza

Nunca imaginaste verte así,
en lo más profundo y oscuro del pozo,
en la destrucción más absoluta,
solo, sin nada,
sin ti.

Destrucción

Zarpazos de desprecio
desgarran el alma
con uñas de ira.

Violencia
que golpea
ridiculiza
sangra
y asfixia.
Duele.

La nauseabunda culpa
hace jirones la vida,
no hay sonrisas
ni cálidas miradas.

Solo confusión
y devastación,
solo aislamiento
y destrucción.

Existencia

Juntos, en esta habitación,
esquivamos nuestras miradas.

Hace mucho tiempo
que no lo intentamos,
que no nos esforzamos
y preferimos vestirnos
con la podredumbre
que hay en el vacío
que nos separa.

Ausentes e invisibles,
permitimos que nuestros días
se diluyan por las grietas
que deja nuestra respiración,
ajena y distante,
en la indiferencia
de la almohada.

Cada vez que encuentro
las marcas de tu presencia,
opto por aceptar la rendición,
y saborear lo incómodo

que es este pantano de emociones
en el que me da miedo nadar,
para salir e intentar respirar.

¿Qué sentido tiene todo?
¿Por qué seguimos aquí?

Las gafas de colores

Decir 'todo está bien'.
Sonrisa desgajada a dentelladas
por el desconcertante rugido del huracán.

Refugio permanente del miedo desdibujado
por las gafas de colores en mis sangrantes ojos.
Fotografía con la que protejo mi realidad coloreada
asegurándome que 'todo está bien', y
'mañana cambiará todo'.

Y así, día tras día, año tras año,
la autoestima es consumida
por palabras incandescentes
que el alma guarda
como si no importaran.

Para cuando tomo consciencia de la realidad,
ya es tarde, soy una sombra invisible,
incluso para mí mismo.
Soledad absoluta en la que sigo repitiéndome:
'todo está bien'.

Las gafas de colores

deberían llamarse
gafas de la inconsciente antonimia voluntaria
y las llevo puestas desde hace mucho más tiempo
del que imaginaba.

Carcoma

¿Los escuchas?
¿Los oyes roer en mi interior?
Horadan la esperanza muerta.

Palabras quebradas los alimentan
en hondos agujeros infectos,
podridos,
Vacíos.

Dentro.

Sonido de madera vieja.
Están ahí,
nunca se van.

Amor infinito

¿Qué haces, hijo?

Leyendo un cuento, papá.

¿Tú sabes que papá es profe de cuentos?

¡Claro!

¿Y te gustaría ser profe también?

No.

¿No? ¿Y qué te gustaría ser?

Quiero ser mago

Pero, ¿en un espectáculo?

Sí, claro.

Pero, a ver, explícame eso.

Los magos hacen magia y por eso
              no pueden morir.

Foto

El sangrante temblor de una notificación
que lo cambia todo para siempre.

Papá, ¿estás llorando?

No hijo,
me han enviado
una foto

muy graciosa.

A

Pelo encrestado que corre alegre
para atrapar el balón. Desde aquí,
mi pecho, ahogado por las lágrimas,
mira con angustia tu carita emocionada,
que grita y anima a los compañeros.

La ansiedad me atraganta
cada bocanada de una realidad que ya no existe,
de un aire que no llega.

Me aferro a la vida por ti.
El mundo como lo conoces pronto desaparecerá.
Intenté evitarlo. No pude. Pero,
¿qué pasará cuando lo sepas?

Cariño, ¿seguirá igual de luminosa tu mente
cuando vea el precipicio al que se asoman
nuestras vidas? ¿Cómo serán tus noches,
cuando yo, insomne, te observe
y tú intentes dormir?

C

Esponjosos abrazos de risa rubia.
La voz brillante de tus ojos nocturnos.
La cara dulce de tus manitas.
Besos llenos de girasoles…

Me paraliza el sufrimiento
que oscurece tu inocencia
cuando me esfuerzo por ocultar
la punzada de mis miedos.

Pero miraremos juntos las estrellas desde la ventana
y te diré lo que siento, serán palabras tiernas
y traerán la frescura de las azucenas.

'Papá, estoy harto de este virus.
Quiero que estemos todos juntos otra vez'.

No es por el virus, mi vida.

Huida

La huida no es salvación,
no lleva a un lugar
donde la luz del sol
calme las palabras,
los besos sequen
los abrasados párpados
o las miradas endulcen
el vacío.

No es el camino,
aunque lo parezca.

Allí no hay curación posible,
solo sombras hambrientas.

Estás aquí

Exhausto y derrotado,
te pido que me salves, ayúdame
porque soy incapaz de restañar
la sangre de las palabras enfurecidas, de iluminar
la sombra abisal de los ojos lacerantes, de acallar
a los perros que ladran en la noche iracunda.

Puedo verte,
estás aquí,
conmigo.

Abrázame en esta destrucción,
dime cómo cierro las grietas de mis lágrimas.

Ayúdame a recoger mis pedazos y ponlos en mis manos.

Te veo,
me escuchas,
Juntos.

Volver a respirar

El punto de partida

Un 'No tienes que darme explicaciones'
fue el punto de partida.

Pero antes había caminado en la noche, con rabia,
buscando herirme y quedar exangüe.

La bocanada de aire vino en la carretera, junto a ti,
mientras conducías hacia el sur.

Yo aún con la mirada perdida,
febril, ido, cogido por el cuello, sacado a la fuerza,
pero adivinando una libertad incipiente
me senté contigo, al sol, en la plaza.
Agradecí tu mirada, tu calma,
no hubo silencios pues todo volvía a ser como antes.
Los grandes amigos siempre escuchan,
siempre comparten.

En la destrucción, tú hiciste el pozo más ancho,
más fácil de escalar, menos oscuro. Tu abrazo
rasgó la fiebre, aflojó mi sonrisa forzada,
me hizo levantar la vista,
descubrir mi nueva vida. Renacer.

6 de enero

Una sonrisa forzada hace que la luz del sol
rasgue los primeros jirones en la niebla.

Duele
todavía
mucho
más.

Hoy comienza una nueva vida.

Me digo a mí mismo:
　　　Lo peor quedó atrás.
　　　Ahí delante te espera
　　　la mejor versión de ti.

Familia

Ahogado, te extiendo mi corazón
para que lo cojas. Tira fuerte,
sácalo del abismo y quema los disfraces
con los que oculto el desprecio.
que ensucia mi alma.

El miedo retumba en la soledad.
Son las piedras que sostenían mi vida
las que hieren mi mente cuando impactan
con mis recuerdos.

Pero, miro hacia arriba buscando el aire
y tus palabras deslían mi laberinto con su amor.
Blancas estrellas enfrían mis alas calcinadas
y serenan el pulso insomne de mis noches.

Lo que tanto tiempo guardé arde ahora
con llamas que sueltan el pasado
y despejan el camino.

Late fuerte

Tus ojos verdes abiertos en la mañana.
Los primeros rayos de luz reflejados en las sábanas.
Olas que rompen amasando dulcemente tu ánimo.
La consciencia de una vida plena.

Late fuerte, inspira hondo
pues las oscuras y masivas murallas
que carcomían tu alma
fueron derribadas con coraje.
Esas ruinas son tu victoria,
¡tu fuerza!

Confía una vez más en ti.
Pon un pie en el suelo y camina,
camina junto a los que estuvieron a tu lado,
junto a los que habrás de conocer,
junto a ti.

No te lo dije, pero
aunque en ocasiones no lo creyeras,
siempre hemos estado juntos.

Emociones

Nuestras emociones
son las cuerdas de
un instrumento musical.
Quietas, mudas, estáticas…

Hasta que viene alguien
y las hace vibrar.

Toca tu música

Wayne W. Dyer. El Cambio.

No tuve ojos para mirarme. No quise quererme.
Altas barreras crecieron en la silenciosa huida.
Muchas. Latentes. Sólidas. Invisibles.
¡Que no entren!

Me diste a Dyer y, esa misma noche, en la cama, lo escribí:
'No te mueras con la música dentro de ti'.

Párpados abiertos. El eco de tu voz despejó la fiebre.
'¡Inunda el mundo con tu música, sácala toda!'.

Y toqué las notas.
La luz que tuve siempre,
detrás de los muros,
solo esperaba a que confiase en ella.
En mí.

Querido Miguel:
        'El cambio está dentro de ti'.

Y me amé.

[38]

Almendros

El universo bajo los almendros.
Tu sonrisa tocándome; sentir la vida
en tus ojos, flores blancas nos arropan,
tu nombre dentro del pequeño bote de cristal que me
regalaste.

Aquella tarde de febrero escribí tu cuerpo con mis manos
mientras exhalabas el susurro que emanaba de las flores
    (una y otra vez)
con tu boca.

Para salvarme

Hyedra de Trivia (Eva Hyedra López).
Amar a una bruja.

Cómo iba a imaginar que aparecerías, que serías tú
quien me descubriera la magnitud del latido profundo
de la tierra y del viento nocturno en los árboles.

'Amar a una bruja no es fácil', me dijiste.
Subestimé tus palabras.

Pensaba que yo sería capaz de ser más fuerte
que tu magia, que podría eclipsar
el secreto de la luna alojado en tu alma.

Me faltó el convencimiento para alcanzar las raíces
que te conectan con el pulso de las fuerzas telúricas.

Aunque nuestros momentos eran distintos,
quise acompañarte volando entre los árboles
pero danzabas con la letanía de la consciencia
y yo acababa de emerger del mar de la fiebre.

'Las brujas somos libres'.

[40]

Eso hizo que deseara que me amaras
'con todas tus vidas,
con todos los misterios
de tu corazón de bruja'.

Cómo iba a imaginar que, para salvarme de mí mismo,
tendría que dejarte marchar.

Cádiz

Desde la bahía, el viento trae caricias de mar
que mojan mi cara. Mi infancia huele a sal,
tiene el brillo plateado de las olas
y el blanco de las paredes encaladas
que suben por la cuesta reflejando
la infinita luz del sur.

Cuando tuve que irme, dejé que los árboles
siguieran moviéndose con el levante
en las laderas de mis recuerdos.

Muchos años después, buscándome a mí mismo,
acudo a tu encuentro. No sé muy bien quién soy
e ignoro la forma en la que me recibirás en la playa.

Apareces delante de mí, al final de la carretera.
Me recoges con cariño.
Me das la fuerza y los ánimos que buscaba.

Este es mi lugar,
mi sitio.

Pliegues

Pliegues de vida a modo de trinchera
desde las que gritar tu locura
enarbolando a Leiva como bandera.

      Como si todo se acabara,
      como si nada importara.

Perder la vergüenza y parar el momento
para defender que estamos juntos
riendo desde las alambradas.

Una fiesta en el desierto,
un concierto prohibido,
un baño sin ropa en Las Vegas.
Poner la vida del revés
cantando sin recuerdos.

El viento hace sonar la música
que da luz a los pliegues de libertad
en tus ojos.

Kitesurf en Tarifa

Brazos tensados de levante con olas
que corren bajo pinceladas pastel en la playa
El susurro de la estela en el azul profundo
lleva palabras que elevan la mente
sobre el mar de Tarifa.

Es el viento que viene del océano,
rizando las crestas de cristal,
quien cauterizó, con sal,
las cicatrices que aún atoraban mi voz.

Las líneas de la cometa se elevan,
lo hacen alto, lo hacen con fuerza,
la que tiene el alma en la punta del sur.

En la playa,
con la tabla bajo el brazo,
la cometa en la mano,
y la mirada en el Atlántico,
nace un nuevo yo.

Noches de sushi

Tus ojos, dibujados por la luna,
se hunden en canciones
bajo las sábanas del confinamiento.

Noches de sushi a la luz de una lámpara de sal
mientras vivimos los pasos de un otoño
que avanza encajonado entre altas paredes de roca.

Somos amantes que exploran, entre las sombras,
el viento que agita las palabras de nuestra realidad,
sin miedos, sin definiciones.

Es la forma que tenemos de liberarnos
de la escarcha que la pandemia deja caer
sobre nuestro ánimo.

Poliamor

'Sé que lo deseas, pero
nunca oirás tu nombre en mis labios,
baby'.

La calma de la nueva vida

Palabras

Son las palabras escritas en diciembre
las que, con botas blancas,
llaman al portal;
dibujan el viento
con el perfume de las sirenas
en la noche densa.

Sin red

En la espiral de notificaciones
estuvimos siempre mucho más cerca.

Buscábamos calmar de la garganta la sed
que deja la procesión de perfiles sin alma.
La agenda roja que nunca para.

Nos quedamos con la muestra.
Colgamos en la puerta
el cartel 'Cerrado por amor'.

Aventuras terminadas.
    Corazón abierto.

    Sin red.

Tengo que decirte

Marea baja para regalarnos
la oportunidad de darnos valor,
de estar.

Tanto nos hemos esperado
que se nos derrama el tiempo
cuando se posa en nosotros
la luz de la tarde.

Placeres indómitos de medianoche
nos devuelven la voz cuando,
tendidos, nos miramos profundamente
y nos decimos:
          Estamos.

Presentación

En la nueva vida,
tu pareja necesita
de la aprobación de los hijos
como tus padres
necesitaron la de tus abuelos.

Mismos nervios.

Fantasmas

Aún siento, a veces,
la sombra de los fantasmas
que salen de mis recuerdos.

Sombras ardientes que,
como lava remanente,
desde el fondo,
calientan los temores
y suben de nuevo
unas décimas la fiebre
rasgando las cicatrices,
paralizando mi ser.

Son esos fantasmas
que creí haber vencido
los que ahora vuelven porque,
en realidad,
ya forman parte de mí.

Tu secreto

En la penumbra de la habitación
te dije que había consumido mi vida
enseñando a los demás.

Pero nunca tuve, a mi lado,
la mirada de la que aprender
el secreto salvaje de las brujas.

Confesión

Amor,
    llenas mi vida
    y llenas mi cama.

Ya no estamos,
    somos.

¡Vive!

Recuerdo que oculté las dentelladas
porque no quería ver el desgarro
que daba de comer a las sombras.

El impacto rompió el disfraz
que vestían los fantasmas
con los cristales sangrantes
del engaño.

Con coraje aprendí a dar luz al sonido
de mis sonrisas y música
al calor de mis miradas.

Fuerza vital para decir
que todo ha valido la pena
para estar aquí,
en este momento
y en este lugar
feliz,
en paz,
conmigo

Aguas tranquilas

No hay espinas en la voz
susurrante del mar
que sale de tu garganta
y llega, como las olas
con su música, blanda a mi piel.

Tocas, con tus manos,
mis sueños esta noche
que sentimos algo fría
pues, ni aún ahora,
la vida es sencilla,
aunque sí más cómoda,
más serena, más amable.

Es la vibración al acercarnos
la que sonroja nuestras bocas
cuando miramos el presente
de nuestras vidas en este mundo,
ahora tan distinto
y tan cercano.

No hay espacio para el rencor,
y hace ya tiempo que estamos en paz

con nuestro pasado.

Aguas tranquilas
que bañan nuestro ánimo y dan lustre
a nuestra victoria frente al miedo.

Aguas tranquilas de calma y amor.

Victoria

Fue necesario arder
para comenzar a respirar.

Y todas estas sombras
no son más que los fantasmas
de la fiebre que nos persiguen,
invaden, atenazan y aterran
mientras crecemos
y aprendemos.

Me sorprendo cuando,
a pesar del sufrimiento,
me veo echando de menos
todo el doloroso proceso
y pienso que, en definitiva,
me ha gustado vivirlo.

Miro lo que he hecho,
lo que he conseguido.

Ahora soy mucho más fuerte,
más libre,
¡mejor!

Soy invencible,
soy imparable,
    soy
    yo.

[64]

Biografía del autor

MIGUEL ÁNGEL GARCÍA GUERRA (San Fernando, 1974) es profesor de Lengua Castellana y Literatura en el Colegio San Juan Bosco, de Torrejón de Ardoz. Licenciado en Filología Hispánica, ha dado clases de Español como Lengua Extranjera en la Cámara Oficial de Comercio de Madrid y en diversos programas educativos internacionales. De 2003 a 2010, fue director académico de Escuela Internacional.

Por otra parte, ha publicado varios artículos en libros y revistas especializadas del mundo educativo y es autor de la serie META ELE (Editorial Edelsa), una colección de libros de texto dedicados a la enseñanza del Español como Lengua extranjera. Su blog educativo fue reconocido con el distintivo 'Buena Práctica 2.0' del INTEF (Ministerio de Educación y Ciencia) y, además, obtuvo el tercer premio del VII Premio Internacional Espiral Edublogs.

Algunas curiosidades sobre el autor: su pasión por las letras y la docencia ha hecho que, en varias ocasiones, haya querido sumergir a sus alumnos de secundaria en la literatura a través de la creación de videojuegos con trasfondo literario, incluso, uno de ellos, ELDERS OF MADNESS, fue expuesto en la Game Developers Conference de San Francisco. También, dirigió el cortometraje LAS BUENAS MANERAS, una historia ambientada en la posguerra española.

Índice

MISLAID DREAMS

IRFAN NAZIR WANI

Made with ♥ on the Notion Press Platform
www.notionpress.com

To the hearts that have loved deeply, lost painfully, and risen quietly.
To those who have wandered through the noise of the world seeking
meaning in silence.
To every soul who has found solace not in worldly applause, but in
the quiet surrender of sujood.

This book is dedicated to you
the seekers of redemption,
the bearers of unspoken wounds,
and the believers who continue to hope,
trusting that even shattered dreams can lead to divine healing.

May your journey be heard, your prayers answered,
and your heart always find its way back to the One who never
abandons **Allah.**

Contents

Foreword

Mislaid Dreams is not merely a novel it is a mirror held up to the human soul. Within its pages lies a deeply emotional journey that explores the delicate threads of love, loss, repentance, and spiritual awakening. Through the life of Zaid, the story speaks to a generation quietly carrying the weight of unmet expectations, broken promises, and the longing for peace that the world often fails to provide.

What makes this book stand out is its ability to transform pain into poetry, silence into strength, and heartbreak into hope. The narrative moves seamlessly from the fast-paced reality of New York to the spiritual serenity of Makkah, offering readers not just a story, but a sanctuary where faith, forgiveness, and healing converge.

In a time when many feel lost in the noise of modern life, Mislaid Dreams reminds us that true sukoon is not found in material success or fleeting affection, but in turning inward toward the soul, and ultimately, toward Allah. Every chapter calls us to reflect, reconnect, and remember that the path to healing often begins in the quiet act of sujood.

This book is a companion for those who have questioned, wept, hoped, and prayed. It is for the dreamers whose paths were diverted but whose spirits remain resilient. May it inspire you, comfort you, and remind you that no dream is truly mislaid when entrusted to the One who never forgets.

Irfan Nazir Wani
Author

Preface

Mislaid Dreams is not just a story it is a reflection of every heart that has once loved, lost, fallen, and longed for redemption. Through the life of Zaid, the book explores the fragile nature of human emotions, the weight of past mistakes, and the deep yearning for divine peace.

*This journey takes readers from the bustling streets of New York to the sacred silence of Makkah, reminding us that while dreams may shatter, the soul can still find healing in sujood. Every chapter is a prayer, every tear a verse, and every word a whisper to the One who always listens **Allah.***

This book is for anyone who has questioned their worth after heartbreak, who has searched for meaning in silence, and who has found sukoon not in the arms of the world, but in the prostration of faith.

Irfan nazir wani

Acknowledgements

Alhamdulillah, all praise belongs to **Allah the One who mends the broken**, *who hears every silent tear, and who gives peace through patience.*

I express my heartfelt thanks to those who walked beside me during the creation of this book. To the quiet souls whose stories live between the lines, and to those who never stopped believing in the healing power of faith you gave this work its depth.

To my family, friends, mentors, and readers thank you for your unwavering support, love, and duas. And to every reader who sees their reflection in Zaid's tears and transformation, this book is yours too.

May Mislaid Dreams remind us that no dream is truly lost when it leads us back to **Allah.**

Irfan Nazir Wani

Prologue

There comes a moment in every soul's journey when the noise of the world begins to fade, and all that remains is the quiet echo of a broken heart and the whispers of what once was. Mislaid Dreams begins at such a moment where hope and regret stand face to face, and the past clings to the present like a shadow.

This is not a tale of perfect endings. It is a story of detours, of paths once bright that turned dim, of promises that dissolved into silence. At its center is Zaid a man who once carried the world in his eyes but now walks through life searching for what was lost: peace, purpose, and the version of himself he left behind.

As readers, we follow Zaid through the bustling chaos of New York, across oceans of memories, and into the sacred stillness of Makkah. His is a story of love that was never fully expressed, of prayers delayed by pride, and of dreams misplaced not by fate alone, but by the choices we make when we are furthest from who we truly are.

But this is also a story of return. Of how even the most broken hearts can be mended. Of how sujood the humblest of acts can lift the heaviest of burdens. It reminds us that redemption is always within reach, no matter how far we've wandered.

Mislaid Dreams is a journey for anyone who has ever loved deeply, failed silently, or wept quietly in the darkness of night. It is for the seekers, the sinners, and the souls who believe that even in ruins, there can be rebirth.

This is not just Zaid's story it is all of ours.

CHAPTER ONE

The Valley's Daughter

"There are silences that don't just linger they scream. That day, when Falak said she didn't want to leave Kashmir, I heard it in her voice: the sound of roots tearing. I wish I had held her hand then, before the city lights could drown her soul." Zaid

The early winter had arrived quietly in the Valley, with soft snowflakes tracing invisible verses in the cold Kashmiri air. The Chinar trees, once ablaze in autumn's glory, now stood bare silent witnesses to change. Morning prayers echoed through the mist as smoke curled from chimneys, mingling with the scent of noon chai and dried spices. The village was hushed, as if holding its breath before a farewell.

In the midst of this serene landscape lived *Falak*, a girl carved from the soil of the mountains and the silence of the snow. Reserved but radiant, she carried a quiet intensity a mind sharp as a scalpel and a heart tender enough to feel the ache of leaves parting from branches. Her teachers called her *"the silent flame,"* a name she had earned through relentless discipline, unmatched academic brilliance, and a grace that never asked for attention but always drew it.

Now eighteen, Falak stood on the edge of a life others had dreamed for her. She had secured admission to **AIIMS,**

Delhi India's most prestigious medical college. What others saw as a triumph, she experienced as a tremor in her soul. For while the world applauded her success, only Falak knew the weight of what it might cost.

And so begins her journey...

"Ammi, I don't want to go to Delhi."

Falak's voice cracked like a brittle twig beneath the weight of unshed tears. She stood by the clay wall of their small but warm kitchen, her long braid brushing against her back, eyes downcast as if afraid that the words she had just spoken might betray the dreams her parents had woven for her.

"I don't like anything outside Kashmir," she added with the tremor in her voice more than just adolescent rebellion. It was the ache of a girl who had learned to breathe in the hush of snowfall, found comfort in the Azaan drifting from distant masjids, and trusted the silent wisdom of Chinar trees that spoke only through their stillness.

Her mother, Yasmeen, turned around, drying her henna-stained hands on her dupatta, and looked straight into her daughter's eyes.

*"Your Abbu spent **sixteen years** in Delhi, Falak. Not for himself but for us. He left the peace of his own home to work in a city that never sleeps, just so you could one day dream beyond these mountains."*

Falak opened her mouth, but did not say anything. Her eyes burned.

*"You've secured admission into **AIIMS Delhi,** the top medical college in India. People pray their whole lives for this opportunity and now that you have it, we're all moving with you there...only because of you,"*

Yasmeen said, her voice suspended between pride and quiet sorrow.

Falak sat down on the small rug, pulling her knees to her chest. The golden glow of the evening sun filtered through the small lattice window, casting patterns on her face soft shadows dancing across the battlefield in her heart.

"Ammi... what if I lose myself there?"
Her voice was barely a whisper, a fragile wisp of a storm she was too young to name.

Yasmeen knelt beside her, gently placing a hand on her head.

"Beta, even roses grow in deserts. You carry Kashmir within you in your akhlaq, in your prayers, in your silences. Don't be afraid of losing yourself. Fear only not blooming at all."

Falak bit her lip, nodding slowly, but the lump in her throat refused to dissolve. She had always been a **brilliant student** topping every exam, memorizing anatomy like poetry, diagnosing illnesses in her siblings before any doctor could. Teachers called her *the silent flame*. But brilliance doesn't protect the heart from breaking when it's asked to say goodbye to everything it loves.

That night, as the whole family gathered for dinner, her Abbu soft-spoken and greying sat beside her.

"I left Kashmir at twenty-one," he said, his voice layered with memories. *"I cried every night for the first year but that pain built the road that brought you here today. Promise me, you will take that road further."*

Falak looked at her parents, at her younger brother Daniyal who was quietly doodling her name on a piece of paper, at the half-eaten roti on her plate, and at the prayer mat folded near the window and then she whispered,

"I will try, Abbu. For you. For Ammi. For Kashmir."
She didn't say "for me" because part of her already knew:

This journey might demand everything. That night, she wrote in her own diary for the first time in months:

"I don't know if Delhi will ever feel like home. But I will walk into it with my spine straight and my faith intact. If I break, I'll break praying. And if I heal... I'll carry that healing back to the Valley."

Outside, a gentle snow had begun to fall. Kashmir, as always, wept quietly.

CHAPTER TWO

Dreams beyond the Mountains

"They say cities are made of lights, but I think they are built on echoes the echoes of the ones who miss their mountains, their lanes, their languages. Falak walked into Delhi with a trembling heart and two suitcases: one for clothes, the other filled with prayers. I watched her from across the corridor, her eyes lost and yet still searching for something familiar. Sometimes, home isn't a place it's a wound that never truly heals." Zaid

The Delhi air was dry, thick with fumes and unfamiliar tongues. Horns never stopped. People moved like currents fast, endless, directionless. For Falak, stepping into the city was like stepping into a storm of sounds, colours, and solitude.

The sky here didn't feel like the one above Srinagar. It was wider but emptier. There were no Chinars. No scent of noon bread. No Azaan flowing across lakes. No Daniyal to hug her when she cried silently into her pillow.

It had only been two days since they arrived. The flat allotted near the medical college was clean but cold not from the air, but from the absence of belonging.

Her parents tried their best to make it feel like home. Yasmeen cooked Falak's favourite Yakhni, but the spices tasted strange, altered by this unfamiliar air. Abdul Hameed hung a poster of Dal Lake in the drawing room. But even printed lakes couldn't still the waves of her restlessness.

Falak stared blankly at her books her name now tagged under one of the top medical colleges in India. She had worked for this, burnt oil till dawn, memorised volumes when other girls were out shopping or on Instagram. Yet now that she was here, something felt... wrong.

The seat was hers. But her soul? It still sat beside her brother in the old wooden house in Srinagar, listening to Kashmiri lullabies as snow kissed the windowpanes.

That evening, her mother knocked softly. **"Falak, should we go for a walk to India Gate?Everyone says it's beautiful."**

Falak shook her head. *"No, Ammi. I'm tired."*

Yasmeen knew that tiredness well. It wasn't of the body. It was the exhaustion of being emotionally displaced. So she said nothing, just kissed her daughter's forehead and left quietly.

The College.

On her first day at the college, Falak wore a simple grey kurta and white scarf. Her eyes scanned the corridors cautiously. Girls were dressed in brands she hadn't heard of. Their conversations floated around things she couldn't relate to parties, salons, cricket matches, boyfriends, and brunch.

She sat in the third row. Alone. Her notebook open, her pen still, her thoughts far from anatomy.

That's when **Zaid** first saw her.

She didn't notice him. But he noticed everything the way she held her pen too tightly, the way she blinked when someone laughed behind her, the way her scarf was pinned perfectly, as though her dignity depended on it.

Zaid had been in Delhi for two years already. A Kashmiri boy, quiet, observant, one who had learned early that survival in cities meant becoming invisible. But the sight of Falak tore something in him.

She looked like she had brought the snow with her.

And for reasons unknown, he couldn't look away.

That evening, he wrote in his diary:

"There are girls who wear makeup to hide themselves. Then there's her a girl who hides herself beneath silence, behind longing. I don't know her name yet. But I know this she doesn't belong here. Not because she's weak, but because she's made of something cities cannot understand."

A week passed.

Falak began to withdraw. She performed well in class but avoided eye contact. She ate alone, spoke little, and left straight after lectures. Every night, she sat quietly, staring at her phone replaying old messages from Daniyal. One voice note of their **cat meowing** made her weep for half an hour.

One night, she asked her mother softly, "Do you think I made a mistake coming here?"

Yasmeen looked at her for a long time. Then said, "No. But I think you're still looking for pieces of yourself you left in Kashmir."

It was raining the day she finally noticed Zaid.

She had forgotten her umbrella, and most students had already left. She stood under a tree, waiting for the downpour to soften. That's when Zaid, walking past with a book in hand, stopped and quietly offered his umbrella.

"No thanks," she said instinctively.

He smiled softly. "It's not a favour. It's just... easier when it's shared."

She looked at him for the first time truly looked. His eyes were kind. His voice wasn't pushy. He looked like someone who knew how to stay quiet in a world too loud.

She hesitated. Then nodded.

They walked silently across the college courtyard. The rain hit the umbrella softly, like an old lullaby.

"Are you from Kashmir?" he asked.

She looked up in surprise.

"Yes. Srinagar."

He nodded. "So am I. Downtown."

Falak paused. Her heart skipped a strange beat.

Something unspoken passed between them the kind of recognition only two displaced souls can feel.

When they reached the gate, she handed back the umbrella.

"Thank you."

He smiled again. "Your name?"

"Falak."

He didn't say his. Just walked away, but with a face she wouldn't forget.

That night, her diary was opened for the first time in weeks. She wrote:

"I met someone today. A stranger with familiar silence. Maybe the city has corners that don't hurt."

And in his own diary, Zaid wrote:

"Falak. Her name means sky. But she walks like she's still trying to find her wings."

From the diary of Zaid:

"Some people walk into your life like a quiet breeze. You don't hear them come, but suddenly, the silence inside you feels less empty. Falak didn't smile much. But the sadness in her eyes spoke a thousand verses. She wasn't lonely. She was just homesick for a place no map could find."

The first semester grew heavier with each passing week.

Anatomy labs. Midnight study sessions. Viva questions that left even the brightest speechless. But none of it scared Falak she had studied through curfews and internet shutdowns back home. She knew what hardship meant.

What she didn't know was how to smile when the loneliness began to ache.

Even in a crowd of 300 students, she felt unseen. A number. A rank. A roll call. Not a person.

Back home in Kashmir, Falak was the star school topper, morning Qur'an reciter, the girl who stitched her brother's torn socks and helped her neighbors with tuition for free. In Delhi, she was **"That quiet Kashmiri girl."**

She missed the Azaan echoing across Nigeen Lake. She missed the smell of kahwa and the sound of her father's slippers on the wooden staircase. She missed snow falling on rooftops like a prayer.

Now, her mornings began with alarms. Cafeteria food. And the hum of metro trains.

Zaid watched her from a distance not to intrude, but to protect, silently.

He knew how the city wrapped itself around your voice and made you forget how to speak.

He had lived those first months alone, hiding tears behind textbooks, calling home only when he could bear the sound of his mother's voice.

That's why he didn't speak much to Falak. But he made sure to sit near her in the library. Share extra notes. Leave a kahwa-flavored tea bag on her desk anonymously.

She never asked who it was. But her lips would curl, just slightly, when she found it.

One afternoon, it all burst open.

Falak had just returned from a three-hour lab when she received a call from home.

Daniyal her little brother had fallen from the staircase. He had fractured his wrist, nothing serious, but the sound of him crying on the phone shattered something inside her.

She locked herself in the college washroom and sobbed. Deep, stifled sobs. Not for the fracture. But for the fact that she wasn't there to hold his hand.

That evening, she didn't go home.

She sat in the garden near the library, face buried in her knees.

Zaid saw her from the distance. He approached slowly, without words, and sat beside her.

They didn't speak.

They didn't have to.

The silence between them was sacred a prayer unspoken, a wound shared.

Finally, she whispered, **"Do you ever stop missing home?"**

Zaid looked straight ahead. **"No. You just grow around the ache."**

She turned to him. "You left Kashmir when?"

"When I was 17 for MBBS. My father wanted me to escape the curfews. But sometimes I think I left my voice there."

Falak blinked slowly. Then said, "I left mine with Daniyal."

And then, for the first time, she smiled not a wide grin, but the kind that escapes between broken things.

Zaid's Diary Entry that Night:

"She cried today. Not loudly. Not with tears. But the kind of crying you do when no one is looking. I sat beside her, and we talked like two trees caught in the same windstorm leaning

quietly, not to break, but to survive. I didn't ask for her trust. I just wanted her to know she wasn't invisible."

Days passed. Falak didn't become talkative overnight, but something began to shift.

She didn't sit alone anymore in the library.

She started bringing two cups of kahwa one for herself, one left near Zaid's usual spot.

She smiled more.

Sometimes, she even laughed when Zaid made dry jokes about professors.

They never talked about love.

They talked about home.

About how hard it is to explain the taste of noon chai to someone who's never had it.

About how even Delhi's winter couldn't imitate the chill of a December night in Kashmir.

One day, she told Zaid, "You know... I don't hate Delhi anymore. But it still doesn't know my name."

Zaid replied gently, "Maybe it's waiting for you to write it on your own terms."

From Falak's private journal that night:
"I thought I had mislaid my dreams somewhere between Srinagar and Delhi. But maybe... they're just changing shape. Maybe Allah doesn't steal from us maybe He just reshapes our grief into something softer. I don't know where this road leads. But tonight, I'm not afraid of walking it."

From the diary of Zaid:
"She doesn't know this yet, but Falak is a poem Allah is still writing. A girl who carries the snow of Kashmir in her silence, and the fire of longing in her heart. Maybe that's why Delhi can't melt her. She was never meant to be ordinary."

The semester crawled forward, leaving behind sleepless nights, phone calls filled with silence, and occasional glimpses of comfort between shared tea and Qur'an verses murmured under trembling breaths.

Falak still missed home but now her ache had a witness.

And that made all the difference.

Zaid had begun waiting for her outside the anatomy hall, not to walk her back, but to be there just in case the world felt too heavy again.

Sometimes he'd say nothing. Sometimes he'd speak about his late father, how grief stays but changes clothes. And sometimes, he'd simply offer her a tissue and a smile.

And Falak? She no longer wore only fear in her eyes.

There were days when her hijab flew in the wind as she laughed at something Zaid said. And days when she wept quietly at the hostel masjid, forehead on the ground, asking Allah to make her strong again.

She wasn't healing completely but she was learning to standup along with the pain.

One evening, as they sat beside the hostel's rooftop, the sky dyed in twilight hues, Falak whispered,

"You know what hurts the most?"

Zaid waited.

"It's not the homesickness. Not the cold classrooms or the loneliness. It's this terrifying fear... that one day, I'll forget what my father's voice sounds like when he calls me gulabo."

Zaid's chest tightened.

He didn't know what to say.

So he said nothing.

And in that silence, her tears fell soft and slow like Kashmir snow melting on Delhi concrete.

From Falak's diary, that night:

"This city may never know the rhythm of my heart. But maybe, just maybe... someone here hears it beating."

CHAPTER THREE

When Two Souls Collide

Falak had always believed in destiny the quiet pull of the unseen that brings people together at the right time, for reasons only known to the stars. She wasn't looking for anyone. Her world was already full with dreams she was chasing, books she was reading, and prayers she whispered under the starlit sky. But fate had its own way of weaving people into the fabric of our lives.

Zaid entered like a breeze soft, effortless, and warm. He wasn't loud like others, nor did he try too hard to impress. That, perhaps, was his charm. He looked away when others looked too long. He smiled when he didn't have to. And he carried a silence that felt like poetry to someone like Falak, who often got lost in her own world.

They met in the college library, of all places. Falak was flipping through a worn-out poetry book, her fingers tracing the underlined verses like prayers. Zaid was sitting across from her, sketching mindlessly into his notebook. Their eyes met once. Just once. And that was enough for a seed to be planted in Falak's heart.

She didn't know him. Not really. All she knew was what he allowed the world to see: a quiet, mysterious boy who never flirted openly, who spoke less, and who looked like he carried an unspeakable past.

But what Falak didn't know was this Zaid was a master of masks.

He wasn't what he seemed. Behind that soft demeanor was a boy who had broken more hearts than he could remember. He had never taken love seriously. In fact, he laughed at the idea of it. To him, emotions were games. Girls were puzzles. And attention was a sport he had mastered.

But with Falak, he didn't play the same way.

Maybe it was her innocence. Maybe it was her sincerity. Or maybe, he just liked the way she looked at him like he was more than he ever allowed himself to be.

Falak began to feel it slowly a tug in her chest when he passed by, a skip in her breath when he smiled, a warmth that bloomed in her veins when he said her name, just once, just softly.

He never told her he loved her.

He didn't need to.

Falak filled the silence between them with her hopes. She mistook his glances as signs, his gestures as feelings, his presence as promise. She started writing poems again, this time with someone in mind. She began praying with more tears. She even smiled more, laughed more, and glowed in a way only girls in love do.

But what she didn't know what she couldn't even imagine was that Zaid had done this before. Many times. With many hearts.

And she was just another story he never intended to finish.

Still, how could she have known? Her heart was untouched. Her soul was unguarded. She believed in what she saw. And she saw a boy who seemed different. Who seemed kind. Who seemed worth the risk.

Sometimes, love doesn't come with red flags. Sometimes it comes like a sunrise—slow and golden and full of promises. And by the time you realize it was an illusion, you've already built a home in its light.

Falak was falling.

And Zaid?

Zaid was watching.

Days turned into weeks, and what began as glances in the library turned into long walks around the campus garden, sitting beneath the chinar trees, and quiet conversations where the world disappeared and it felt like only they existed.

Zaid knew how to play the game. He gave just enough to make her believe. He wasn't overly romantic no grand gestures, no flashy words but he understood emotions like a puppeteer understands strings.

He spoke in riddles. He spoke in *shayari*.

Every time Falak looked into his eyes and asked what was behind his silence, he'd drop a line that broke her heart and she mistook the break as love.

"Tum meri tanhaayi ho, jise har raat chhupke se chahta hoon,

Magar subah hone tak tum khwab ban jaati ho."

Falak would listen, eyes brimming with tears, thinking he carried a depth that no one else saw. She felt honored that he was letting her in into his brokenness, into his mystery.

But it was all an act.

Zaid had recited those same *shayari* to other girls, with the same pauses, the same tragic voice, and the same distant gaze. He had rehearsed every word, every breath. He knew exactly what to say to stir the heart of someone like Falak.

Yet, Falak saw none of it. She believed. She believed in his pain, in his story, in his silence.

One evening, as they sat beneath a fading sky, she whispered, almost too softly, "Why do I feel like I've known you forever?"

Zaid looked at her, paused, and replied in his calm voice,
**"*Shayad meri taqdeer mein likha tha tum se milna,*
Warna itna khubsurat gumaan toh sirf duaon mein hota hai."**

Falak lowered her eyes, a shy smile blooming on her face, while her heart ached with the beauty of it all.

She was falling. Deeply, completely, recklessly.

And Zaid?

He was smiling inside not because he loved her, but because he knew **he had won her trust.**

He started spending more time with her not because he wanted to, but because drama needs an audience. He sent her voice notes of poems at midnight, shared pictures of old, dusty books, talked about pain he had never really felt.

**"*Main toot gaya hoon, Falak... bahut andar se.*
Kisi ne sach pyaar nahi kiya mujhse... shayad isliye main khud se bhi door ho gaya hoon."**

And she cried for him. Prayed for him. Wrote his name in her diary with trembling hands and whispered, "Ya Allah, uske dard ko mera bana de..."

What she didn't realize was:

He wasn't broken.

He was **empty.**

Empty of sincerity, empty of truth, but full of cleverness.

And while Falak was writing his name in her prayers, he was already preparing to **disappear** from her story when the time felt right.

But for now, the show must go on.

And Falak?

She was still holding on to the lie like it was the only truth that ever mattered.

Months slipped by like the pages of an old diary caught in the wind. What began as hesitant steps between two strangers became long conversations, shared sunsets, whispered poems, and days that Falak believed were written by fate itself.

She didn't notice how the seasons changed, how the chinar leaves turned golden and then bare, only to bloom again. All she noticed was **Zaid**—his silence, his words, his wounds, his world.

He became her everything.

And in that everything, she lost herself.

Each evening, when the college corridors emptied and the lights dimmed, he would walk beside her in silence sometimes speaking in fragments of Urdu poetry, sometimes with nothing at all.

"Tum samundar ho Falak... aur main sirf ek lehar jo kabhi laut ke na aaye..."

And she would write those words in her journal, thinking they were his truth.

But Zaid... Zaid wasn't building a future. He was performing.

And yet, **she trusted every emotion he pretended to feel**.

What she didn't see was the way he checked his phone after they parted, how his tone shifted in other conversations, how his charm was **not hers alone**—but a mask he wore with different faces.

Months turned into years.

Falak was in her second year now. Zaid had reached his final.

He had grown quieter less poetry, more distraction. She noticed he took longer to reply, smiled a little less, and avoided deep talks. But she thought maybe life was pressuring him, maybe his career weighed heavily on his shoulders.

Still, her love didn't waver. She brought him notes, waited outside his department building, sent him late-night duas, and whispered his name in her tahajjud prayers.

"Ya Allah, agar mera Zaid sach hai... toh uske dil mein bhi mere liye mohabbat paida kar..."

But Allah listens to hearts, not lies.

Zaid was already pulling away.

Slowly. Quietly.

Like a thief exiting a house he had once stolen light from.

In his final semester, he had already begun planning his departure—not just from the college, but from her life.

He didn't say much anymore. And when he did, it was distant, like echoes in an abandoned room.

Falak would ask, *"Kya main tum par bojh ban gayi hoon, Zaid?"*

And he'd reply with a sigh and a half-hearted smile:

"Nahi Falak... par kabhi kabhi, kuch cheezein khud se door ho jaati hain... be wajah..."

She nodded, smiled, and cried the moment he turned away.

She still believed in their story.
Still held onto the hope that this silence was temporary.
That he would return more loving, more real.

But the truth was:

Zaid was never real.

He was a passing storm, and Falak...
Falak was the tree that stood still, thinking the wind had fallen in love with her leaves.

The Promise of Forever

In the quiet corners of campus life, where benches held secrets and gardens bore witness to unsaid words, **Falak and Zaid** continued to write a story one that only **Falak** truly believed in.

Zaid was now in his final year, and though his presence had begun to fade like ink on an old love letter, Falak still clung to the moments that felt like eternity.

He would smile faintly, speak less, yet when he did, it was like a flame flickering just long enough to keep her hope alive.

One evening, as the winter mist curled around the trees, Zaid said softly,

"Main chala bhi gaya... toh tum toh yaad rahogi. Tum jaisi koi nahi hai, Falak."

She held those words close to her heart, like pearls scattered in the sand. She whispered them into her pillow at night, replayed them in her mind during lectures, and carved them into the walls of her future.

They began talking about *forever*.

What city they would live in.

How many books their little library would hold.

What kind of home they would build together.

How her name would sound beside his.

He spoke in metaphors. She believed in promises.

"Ek din tumhara naam mere ghar ke darwaze pe hoga, Falak," he said.

"Aur mere dil pe toh kab ka likha ja chuka hai," she replied.

She didn't know that **his words were scripted, but her emotions were sacred.**

He gave her poems that he didn't write. Shayari that sounded like heartbreak but was hollow within. Words that once made her cry in awe... were perhaps whispered to others before her too.

Still, **she dreamed.**

She dreamed of Zaid in a white kurta, standing beside her in a nikkah ceremony where her eyes would brim with tears of joy.

She dreamed of early mornings making tea for two.

She dreamed of being his calm in a storm, his light in every darkness.

Her diary was filled with his name.

Her prayers were full of his future.

And her heart was too blind to see the cracks beneath his smile.

Zaid?

Zaid was simply performing playing the part of a man she needed, while planning an exit that would shatter everything.

But she didn't know that yet.

She still believed.

Still waited.

Still wove dreams of **"us"** around a man who never really meant to stay.

CHAPTER FIVE

Cracks in the Facade

Time, once a silent witness to their whispered promises, now began to pull them apart.

Zaid was no longer the boy who waited at the library gate or called to recite a verse of heart-wrenching shayari. His presence became rare, and his voice once drenched in affection began to dry into excuses.

One evening, as autumn leaves rustled outside and Falak sat nervously clutching her phone, **he finally said the words she wasn't prepared for:**

"Falak... mujhe US jaana hoga. Ek achhi naukri ka mauqa hai... paison ke liye. Future ke liye."

Her heart thudded.
Not because he was leaving but because it sounded like a goodbye wrapped in ambition.

"Zaid," she said quietly, "Mummy-Papa keh rahe hain ab Nikkah ki baat karo. Main... main chahti hoon ki tum unse baat karo."

She paused, waiting.
Hoping he'd say yes.
Hoping he'd say, *"Main kal hi baat karta hoon, Falak."*

But Zaid took a long breath, then looked away as if her dreams were too heavy for him to carry.

"Abhi nahi, Falak. Main US jaa raha hoon... wahan se sab kuch theek karenge. Sab hoga... bas abhi nahi."

That "abhi nahi" shattered something inside her.

Because she had **waited too long**, **hoped too much**, **loved too deeply**.

But still... she smiled.

"Thik hai... wahan se baat kar lena. Bas jhoot mat bolna kabhi," she whispered.

He said nothing.

What she didn't know was that **Zaid had already decided to exit quietly**. He had played his part too well the emotional shayari, the stolen glances, the made-up dreams — all a curtain to hide his truth.

He didn't want to face his family.

He didn't want to marry her.

He only wanted to disappear... with a fake promise and a broken girl behind.

Falak stood by the window that night, looking at the stars as if they could answer the ache in her chest. She wanted to believe him. She wanted to believe that the US was a temporary distance. That love, real love, would survive.

But deep inside her trembling soul, a voice whispered:

"If he loved you, he would have stayed."

And yet, she waited.

Because sometimes, the most innocent hearts are the last to let go.

Weeks passed. Then months.

Falak counted the days like prayer beads.

Every morning began with a hopeful glance at her phone, and every night ended in silent tears when no message came.

Zaid had left.

He had flown across oceans, promising to return, promising a future.

But what he left behind was a heart wrapped in illusions and stitched together with false hope.

In America...

The city lights of New York were nothing like the soft twilight of Kashmir. The skyscrapers didn't smell like home, and the faces were unfamiliar, but **Zaid didn't mind.**

He had secured a position in one of the **top hospitals of America** a dream job, a dream salary, a dream life.

But unlike Falak, he had never lived for love. He lived for ambition, for admiration, for the applause that echoed in hospital corridors when he walked past as *"Dr. Zaid Khan from India."*

No one here knew about Falak.

No one here asked about the girl who wore an invisible mangal sutra of faith and waited for his call.

Here, Zaid was free.

Free from responsibilities.

Free from expectations.

Free from the innocent girl whose soul he'd touched only to walk away as if it meant nothing.

He smiled at nurses.

He dined with interns.

He attended medical conferences in well-cut suits and perfect smiles.

But not once did he call.

And **Falak**, thousands of miles away, still sent him little messages:

"Hope you're eating well..."

"Did you talk to your parents yet?"

"I miss your voice... your shayari..."

But the *blue ticks* stayed silent.

The boy who once recited verses like:
"Main bewajah nahi roya karta hoon,
Kisi yaad ne zaroor dil toda hoga..."
...had now turned into a silence louder than betrayal.
Back in Kashmir...
Falak clutched her dupatta close, sitting near the heater with her mother busy sewing beside her.
"Did Zaid call today?" her mother asked casually.
She forced a smile.
"Nahi... busy hoga."
But inside, she was breaking.
Because love, when one-sided, becomes a slow death. And she was dying one heartbeat at a time... still wrapped in the lie that he would come back.

CHAPTER SIX

The Waiting Wounds

Two years had passed.

Twenty-four months of waiting.

One thousand and forty-three nights of unanswered prayers.

And a thousand times Falak had opened Zaid's old messages just to read the same fake promises over and over again.

He was still in America.

He still hadn't spoken to his parents.

And Falak... she was now in her **final year of university**, standing at the edge of a new chapter, but stuck in the torn pages of the past.

At home, the pressure had begun to tighten like a noose.

Her mother would mention it softly at first:

"Falak beta... you're in your final year. We must start looking for a suitable boy."

Her father would cough and look away, but his silence carried weight.

Her brother Amir, more direct:

"You've always said next year. That year has come, Falak. Don't lose a good proposal waiting for someone who doesn't even call."

But Falak... she would just lower her eyes, breathe deeply, and whisper,

"Next year, please... not now."

She lied with a soft voice.

But inside, she screamed in confusion why had Zaid not spoken yet?

Why had he gone so quiet after promising forever?

Still, her heart made excuses for him.

"Maybe he's busy."

"Maybe he wants to settle before telling his parents."

"Maybe he still loves me but can't express it."

The girl who once laughed like a river now sat quietly by windows, writing diary entries instead of texting.

She still had his old voice notes the fake, poetic shayari he once whispered at midnight, pretending they came from his own heart:

"Tujhse juda hokar bhi, tujhmein hi rehna hai...
Mohabbat ka yeh waada, waqt se kehna hai..."

But time had become her biggest enemy.

It moved forward, but her heart remained frozen in the past.

And Zaid...

In New York, Zaid was living a double life.

He posted about medical achievements, brunches, and city lights his smiles more perfect than his lies.

He had convinced himself that **ghosting Falak was kinder than saying the truth** that he had never intended to make her his forever.

But love isn't something you just walk away from.

Unless it was never love to begin with.

Falak waits, her heart heavy with silence and unanswered questions.

Days turned into months.
Months turned into years.
But love real love doesn't count time.
It counts silences.
And Falak had heard too many.

She was in her final year now more mature, quieter, and more tired than ever before.

Zaid had changed.

He no longer picked up her calls like he used to.
The boy who once waited desperately to hear her voice now left her messages on **"read"** — for hours... sometimes days.
And when he did respond, his replies were short, distant... cold.

"Busy."
"In a meeting."
"Will call later."

But he never called.

One evening, she had to borrow her cousin's number to call him — just to check if he was okay.
He picked up on the first ring, laughing loudly before realizing it wasn't who he thought.

"Hello? Who's this?"
"Zaid... it's me. Falak."

The line went silent.

Then came the excuse:

"Oh... hey. Sorry, I thought it was someone else. I'm just... really busy lately. Let's talk later, okay?"

He hung up before she could even say *I miss you*.

Far away in America, **Zaid had found a new life.**
A life without waiting.
Without Falak.

He had joined one of the top hospitals in the U.S., as he always dreamed.

But along with success came the **nightlife, the parties, the glittering lie of freedom.**

He had started **dating new girls**, pretending again new poetry for new names.

Falak's love had become a **burden**, a **guilt**, a **reminder** of the boy he used to be.

So he changed her name in his contacts...

Not as "Falak ♥?"

Not even "F."

But just one word:

"Tension."

A name that broke every promise he ever made.

Meanwhile, Falak still believed.

She still thought maybe he's overwhelmed. Maybe he needs time. Maybe... maybe...

But how many "maybes" does it take to finally realize the truth?

Every time she sat on her prayer mat, she wept.

"Ya Allah... if he is mine, return him.

But if he's not... please don't let my heart break loudly."

But her heart was already breaking quietly.

Like glass in velvet.

At university, her friends started noticing her fading laughter.

She stopped wearing bright colors.

Her eyes always looked like she hadn't slept because she hadn't.

Love letters had turned into silent tears.

Calls into unread messages.

And dreams into doubts.

She didn't tell anyone...

But sometimes, even the strongest girls begin to question their worth.

Falak waits, her heart heavy with silence and unanswered questions.

The long hospital corridors at **AIIMS Delhi** were always filled with footsteps, emergencies, cries of new life, and whispers of dying breath.

But somewhere in that chaos, **Falak was crumbling silently inside.**

She had finally entered the **last phase of her MBBS internship**, wearing the white coat she once dreamed of but her hands trembled.

Not because of the patients...

But because of the messages she stopped receiving.

One evening, after a 24-hour shift, her phone buzzed.

It was **Zaid.**

Not a call.

Just a text.

"Can we talk?"

Her heart leapt. She stepped away from the ward, hands shaking, and dialed immediately.

He picked up.

No poetry in his voice. No softness.

Just silence.

"Zaid...?"

"Falak," he sighed, "**I've been thinking.**"

She froze.

"I can't leave my dreams for you."

"What...?" Her voice cracked.

"I worked too hard to get here. I can't come back now. Not for marriage. Not yet."

There was a pause... then the final dagger:

"Right now, I can't marry you."

It felt like someone had knocked the air out of her lungs.

"You promised me... you said—"

"I know what I said," he cut in, "but we were younger then. Things change. People change."

Her knees gave way. She slid to the cold floor of the hospital hallway, her stethoscope still around her neck... her dreams crashing beside her.

"So what was I?" she whispered.

"A pause?"

"A distraction until you reached America?"

Zaid didn't answer.

He didn't need to.

Because silence once again became louder than love.

That night, she cried not just for him.

She cried for **every prayer**, every fast she kept, and every **nafil namaz** she had offered with his name on her lips.

She had stitched his name in her *Duas* and now it hung there... **like a betrayal.**

She stared at the ceiling, whispering:

"Ya Allah... why did I love him so much?

Was it a test? Or a punishment?"

Her phone screen was still lit.

Zaid's name blinked above the message history.

Still saved as **"Tension."**

Still unanswered.

And now, finally...

unwanted.

CHAPTER SEVEN

New Paths, Old Wounds

The snow-capped peaks of Kashmir welcomed Falak back like a distant echo of her childhood dreams a landscape of beauty and silence, where every breath felt heavy with memories.

After graduating from **AIIMS Delhi**, she returned home not with the joy she once imagined, but with a heart fractured beyond repair.

Her father had retired, and the family decided to settle in their ancestral home in **Srinagar**. The familiar streets and crisp mountain air could not erase the ache inside her.

Falak tried to reach out to Zaid one last time but his number was blocked.

His silence was louder than any goodbye.

Her messages remained unread, unanswered.

He had moved on or so it seemed.

Meanwhile, life marched forward.

Falak joined the **MS program at SKIMS, Soura Srinagar** dedicating herself to medicine, healing others even as her own soul bled quietly.

But no amount of work could mend the void Zaid had left behind.

And then, the news came her parents had arranged a marriage for her.

To a doctor she had never met.

The proposal was swift, the conversations brief.
The groom's name was unknown to her, and his face a stranger's.

Falak nodded silently, though inside a storm raged.

She was still deeply, hopelessly in love with Zaid the man who had promised forever but left her alone with broken dreams.

A man who had shattered not only her heart but the hearts of many girls before her each one another casualty of his false promises and lies.

She wondered bitterly if she was just one more name in his long list of betrayals.

Yet, the path was laid before her, like a road she never chose to walk.

Her heart whispered no, but her lips remained silent.

How could she speak of shattered trust when the world expected her to smile, to move on, to heal?

Kashmir's serene mountains stood witness to her pain, and though she donned the white coat of a healer, inside, the wounds of love festered, aching for a closure that might never come.

CHAPTER EIGHT

The Wedding of Withered Dreams

The air was thick with celebration, but inside Falak's heart, there was only silence a suffocating, endless silence.

Her wedding date was finalized.

The invitations had gone out, the arrangements were in place, and the entire house was glowing in joy.

But not her.

Not Falak.

She stood quietly behind the curtain of expectations, wearing a **deep red bridal lehenga**, laced with golden threads the very same shade she once dreamt of wearing for **Zaid**.

Her hands were adorned with **mehndi**, deep and rich, stretching from her fingertips to her forearms. The names of the unknown groom were hidden in intricate designs.

But Falak searched only for **one name** Zaid.

She stared at her hands, turning them over again and again, hoping foolishly, hopelessly that somewhere, hidden in the mehndi lines, she might find his name.

The name that had once made her heart race, the name that now brought only tears.

She called him.

Again.

And again.

But like every night before there was no answer.

Blocked.

Ignored.

Forgotten.

She cried herself to sleep for weeks, her soul collapsing beneath the weight of unspoken grief. The light in her eyes had dimmed, her smile long lost in the pages of her past. Even her parents noticed the hollowness in her laughter but they mistook it for nervousness, not heartbreak.

The night before the wedding, Falak sat in the quiet corner of her room, **her diary in her lap** the one Zaid had gifted her years ago, covered in pressed flowers and memories.

She opened to the page where he had once written:

"Falak, I will never let you go.
Not even if the oceans rise between us.
I will say 'Qabool Hai' with trembling lips,
And you will say it back and that day,
My world will finally be whole."

Tears dropped onto the ink, smudging the words as if even the paper could not hold his lies anymore.

She raised her trembling hands to the sky, her palms red with mehndi and sorrow.

"Ya Allah...
If this is love, then let me forget it.
Let Zaid feel the same pain I feel now.
Let him taste the silence he gave me.
He left me in the middle of the sea
when I needed him the most.
For money, for career, he chose the world.
And I? I chose him over everything."

She sobbed silently, her voice shaking with grief,

"Ya Allah... remove from him the sukoon he stole from me.
Let my tears become his night's burden.
Let my heartbreak echo in his heartbeat."

The next day arrived the wedding day.

The house was filled with laughter, songs, and women whispering about how beautiful the bride looked.

But **Falak's eyes were heavy.**
Each step she took felt like walking barefoot on shattered glass.

She sat quietly in front of the mirror as they placed the dupatta on her head her heart screaming Zaid's name even as her lips stayed silent.

The **Molvi Sahib** arrived.

The air turned solemn, sacred.

And then the words came.

"Falak bint Khalid, Qabool Hai?"

In that moment she froze.

Her mind was not in that room it was **year's back,** beneath the trees of Delhi, when Zaid had once whispered:

"The day I say 'Qabool Hai' to you, and you say it back,
That day will be the most beautiful day of my life."

That memory struck her like lightning.

Reality blurred.

Her lips trembled.

Her eyes widened.

And then **she collapsed.**

The room fell into chaos.

Women screamed.

The Molvi paused.

Falak lay motionless, her body crumpled under the weight of broken promises and unbearable grief.

They rushed her to the hospital the same hospital where she had once dreamed of saving lives.
But this time it was hers that slipped away.

The doctor looked at the monitor and then at her weeping father.

Cardiac arrest.

She's gone.

She left the world with **mehndi still dark on her hands,** and **tears on her lashes.**

She left without saying *"Qabool Hai".*
Because she had already said it
to someone who **never deserved it.**

She left with a **smile painted in pain,**
with **Zaid's name still written on her soul,**
with her **diary closed,** but her dreams **forever mislaid.**

? Some love stories never get closure. Some promises stay buried with the one who believed in them the most. And some people... only understand love after it's gone.

CHAPTER NINE

The Mirage of Love

"And of His signs is that He created for you from yourselves mates that you may find tranquility in them, and He placed between you affection and mercy..."
Surah Ar-Rum (30:21)

Years passed...

Zaid had immersed himself in the fast-paced life of **New York City**, drifting farther from his past in Kashmir. He had everything luxury, freedom, and the attention of many. His days were filled with dates and distractions. Love was a game to him, nothing more.

The Arrival of Hayat

But *one winter afternoon,* **destiny walked in wearing a white coat and a black hijab.**

She introduced herself to the hospital not with words, but with silence and grace.

Her name was **Dr. Hayat Siddiqui**.

Hayat was soft-spoken, calm, and covered in modesty from head to toe. A silent storm of sincerity. While others gossiped and flaunted, Hayat carried the Quran in her heart and humility in her stride.

"Verily, in the remembrance of Allah do hearts find rest."

Surah Ar-Ra'd (13:28)

She was not just another doctor; she was a healer of souls.

One day, a critical surgery came up. A patient had **only a 10% chance of survival**. Even Zaid stepped back. **"I can't,"** he said.

The hospital held its breath.

But Hayat didn't flinch.

She took the case.

With the hands of faith and the heart of a warrior, she navigated through the impossible and saved the patient.

The entire hospital applauded.

Zaid was stunned.

Who was she?

"She is Hayat... Life."

A colleague whispered to Zaid later, "She's from Kashmir. Topper from AIIMS Delhi. Known all over India."

Zaid's ego stiffened.

"She doesn't even talk to me."

"You ever wondered what her name means?" the friend replied. **"Hayat means life.** Maybe she isn't the type of girl who entertains boys who waste theirs."

Zaid's curiosity turned into obsession.

He began to notice everything.

She sat during lunch reading the Quran.

She prayed in the quietest corners of the hospital.

She never engaged in small talk or flirtation.

She lived **with Allah in her heart and no space for anything temporary.**

The First Rejection

One day, during a hospital lunch hour, **Dr. Mehak**, Hayat's friend, came to the cafeteria. Zaid casually approached her, "Hello, Dr. Mehak. How are you?"

She looked at him cold and distant and walked away.

Zaid was stunned.

"What did I do?"

Later, he overheard someone say, "That's Hayat's friend. She knows about your past. Word travels fast."

Something stung inside him.

For the first time, a woman didn't just reject him she made him **question himself.**

Over time, Hayat and Zaid occasionally exchanged salaam.

But she remained distant, untouched by his presence.

Then, in a prestigious hospital meeting, Hayat was introduced to all:

"This is Dr. Hayat Siddiqui. Top graduate from AIIMS, one of the finest cardiologists from Kashmir. We are honored to have her."

Zaid's heart skipped.

"She's from Kashmir... just like me."

He wanted to tell her everything.

His past. His pain. His shame. His change.

But fear froze him.

After the bitter taste of rejection from mehak on that day, Zaid couldn't help but feel a strange restlessness inside him. Something about Hayat pulled at his conscience her presence was graceful, calm, unlike anyone he had ever encountered in his fast-paced, shallow life. Every time he saw her, draped in her modest hijab, immersed in patient care or quietly reciting the Qur'an in the hospital's prayer room, he felt a tug at his heart a feeling he hadn't known before. Not lust. Not a fleeting crush. Something deeper. Something unsettling.

One evening during the hospital's tea break, Zaid finally gathered the courage to speak with Hayat. He spotted her sitting in a quiet corner of the cafeteria, a cup of chai in her hand, reading a small booklet of supplications.

He walked up hesitantly, heart thudding. *"As-salamu Alaikum, Dr. Hayat,"* he said, voice soft and uncertain.

Hayat lifted her gaze briefly, offered a polite but distant *"Wa Alaikum Assalam,"* and lowered her eyes again.

Before he could say another word, Mehak Hayat's colleague and longtime friend appeared by her side. She smiled politely at Zaid, then turned to Hayat. "Come, let's get back to the ward. There's a new case coming in."

And just like that, she left. No smile. No small talk. No interest.

Zaid stood there frozen, the half-empty chair across from him echoing louder than words ever could.

He tried again days later, finding her in the hospital library, reading through a cardiology journal. *"Do you mind if I sit?"* he asked, trying to sound casual.

Hayat didn't even look up. "Sorry, I prefer to study alone."

Another time, he offered to assist her during a complex procedure, but she refused with quiet firmness. *"I already have support staff. Thank you, Dr. Zaid."*

She was not rude. She was not dramatic. She was simply... unavailable. Untouchable. As if a protective wall surrounded her, and he was always on the outside, a shadow at best.

Zaid began to feel like a stranger in his own life. The man who once thrived on admiration now stood invisible in the presence of a woman who saw through him.

For Hayat, Zaid was just another colleague. Nothing more.

And for Zaid... she was slowly becoming everything.

One day, he gathered the courage to greet her in the canteen.

"Asalamu Alaikum, Dr. Hayat."

She looked up, her eyes calm, and replied with grace: *"Wa Alaikum Salaam."*

Then she left, taking the air from his lungs with her.

Days turned to weeks. Unknowingly, Zaid began to change. No more late-night parties. No more meaningless relationships. He found himself waiting for small moments seeing her in meetings, listening to her speak at conferences. The more he denied it, the deeper he fell.

Months passed.

Then, during an Eid gathering, he was invited to her home with colleagues. He met her family her father's proud smile, her mother's tender adjustments of Hayat's dupatta, the way Hayat laughed softly at her brother's jokes.

In that simplicity, Zaid realized he had fallen in love. **Truly. Selflessly. Painfully.**

He wanted to tell her. To confess that he had changed. That he wasn't the Zaid who once played with hearts. That her silence had made him listen to his soul.

The Slow Unraveling

After that Eid gathering, something shifted between them.

Hayat began acknowledging Zaid's presence—not with warmth, but with a quiet courtesy. A nod in the hallway. A brief exchange about patients. Sometimes, if the canteen was empty, she would even sit at the same table, sipping her tea while he pretended not to stare at the way her lashes cast shadows on her cheeks when she looked down.

"I measure my life now in stolen glances,
in the space between her 'hello' and 'goodbye,'
in the way my pulse stutters
when she says my name."

Zaid knew he was slipping.

The late-night parties had stopped. The flirty texts to other women had ceased. Even his colleagues noticed **"Sheikh, you've gone quiet. Who's the unlucky girl who finally tamed you?"**

But Hayat? She remained untouched. Unreachable.

The Descent into Madness

He started noticing things:

The way she tucked a loose strand of hair behind her ear when concentrating.

The faint scent of rosewater that lingered in the elevator after she left.

The small scar on her left wrist from a childhood accident she once mentioned offhand.

Each detail was a knife twisting deeper.

One night, drunk on loneliness, he did something reckless—he typed out a message:

"What would it take for you to see me? Not as I was, but as I am now?"

He deleted it. Rewrote it. Deleted it again.

"I have become a beggar,
holding out my empty hands,
hoping she'll fill them
with something more than pity."

The Day the World Ended

Then, over lukewarm hospital coffee, Hayat shattered him.

"My parents have fixed my engagement. To Ayaan my cousin. We'll be returning to Kashmir next year."

The words hit like a physical blow. Zaid's fingers tightened around his cup, the heat searing his skin, but he felt nothing.

"Funny how the heart keeps beating
even when it's been told
it's no longer allowed to hope."

The Confession He Couldn't Hold Back

The next day, he cornered her in an empty corridor.

"Hayat, I need you to know
I love you. Not as a game. Not as a conquest.
But in a way that terrifies me."

Her expression didn't change. *"Zaid, you don't even know me."*

"I know enough. I know your kindness. Your strength. The way you"

"Stop." Her voice was firm. *"I'm not one of your poetry verses. I'm a woman who honors her word. And my word was given long before you decided to rewrite your story."*

She walked away, leaving him standing there, a man reduced to a footnote in her life.

Weeks passed.
Zaid couldn't breathe. Couldn't sleep.

He picked up a pen... and **wrote a diary with his own blood.**
Each page a testimony to a love that shattered him.
He handed it to Hayat.

When she read it, she cried.

"Zaid... this is insane. Why would you do this?"
"Because I loved you more than myself."
She returned it and whispered:

"You love me. But I love Allah more. And that's why... this can never be."

CHAPTER TEN

The Dream That Burned the Soul

The air inside the hospital grew heavier for Zaid with each passing day. After Hayat's calm but final rejection

"I'm not like the women you've met before. I know your past, Zaid. I've heard the stories... and I cannot betray the trust of my parents. My heart isn't meant for you."

Something shattered within him.

But Zaid, the man once worshipped by admiration and pride, could no longer carry the weight of silence.

He bled for her quite literally.

One evening, when the moon sat low in the night sky and the city of New York buzzed in its usual chaos, he wrote **a letter with his own blood** words drenched in pain, regret, and silent cries. He gave that letter to mehak and ask her to give it to hayat. No expectations. No hope. Just truth.

"Dear Hayat..."

"I once lived with pride in my chest. Now I walk with a heart made of ashes.

You are the only voice my silence listens to, the only peace my chaos seeks.

I don't write this hoping for love... I write it to say I've

changed because of you.
May Allah grant you joy even if it's not through me. But know this
I will never touch another soul with the love I once saved for you."

When Hayat read the blood-stained pages, her hands trembled.
Tears slipped down her cheeks, yet her voice remained firm:

"This is not love, Zaid. This is punishment. I respect your feelings, but I am not the one for you. My heart... was never yours."

A week later, Hayat left New York permanently.
She returned to Kashmir to marry her cousin, a professor at the university a choice arranged by her family, one she accepted with grace and without complaint. She never looked back.

Zaid did.
Again and again.
Each moment she had walked past him now echoed louder than her absence.

The Days without Her

Zaid couldn't bear the hospital corridors anymore every hallway held her scent, every room her presence.
He took extended leave.
Stopped socializing.
His eyes lost their spark; his laughter turned to silence.
He started skipping meals.
He stayed awake for nights staring at the ceiling, begging for sleep that never came or when it did, came with curses.

The Dream

One night, after weeks of emotional collapse, Zaid finally passed out from exhaustion.
And in that fragile sleep, **he saw her**.

But it wasn't Hayat.
It was **Falak** Hayat's closest friend.
Standing in the middle of a dark valley, wearing a bridal dress soaked in rain, tears flowing endlessly.

Her kohl was smudged, her lips trembling. She whispered into the sky:

"Ya Allah... as You are Just, make him feel the ache I have buried.
Let Zaid taste the pain he once gave, let his soul tremble in helplessness...
Just as mine did when he broke hearts like paper."

Zaid jolted awake, his chest pounding.
He could still hear the echoes of her voice...
He could still see her white bridal dress, now crimson with grief.

That dream was not a dream.
It was a **verdict**.

The City No Longer Held Him

Months passed.
Zaid tried to drown in his routine, tried to revive the playboy he once was — but the mirror only showed a haunted face.

New York the city that once gave him wings now suffocated him.
Every face reminded him of the one he lost.
Every callous laugh reminded him of the sins he

committed.

Every prayer he skipped once, now echoed in his ears like chains.

He stood one night at Brooklyn Bridge, watching the water flow silently under the stars.

And he whispered to himself:

**"I came here chasing freedom,
But I found my cage in love.
It is not Hayat who punished me...
It was Allah who loved me enough to make me taste what I gave."**

Decision

Unable to find peace, unable to face her absence, unable to fight the guilt that now lived within his bones.
Zaid packed his bags.

He left his apartment.
He resigned from the hospital.
He booked a one-way flight **not to Kashmir,**
But to **Saudi Arabia** hoping to drown his pain at the feet of the **Kaaba,**
to seek forgiveness in the streets of **Madina,**
to ask Allah to turn his heartbreak into healing.

Because when the world abandons you
only the Creator can revive your soul.

From Zaid's Diary

**"Main woh laash hoon jo saans toh leta hai,
Par zindagi mein kisi ka noor nahi rehta hai.
Uski ek nazar chahiye thi zinda rehne ke liye,
Ab toh har subah bhi maut si lagti hai."**

"Qismat ne usse le jaaya,
Gunahon ne mujhse uska chehra chhupaaya.
Ab har sajda ke baad, sirf ek dua hai
Ya Allah, jo dard diya, usi mein maghfirat chhupa de."

Final Diary Entry in New York

(Before Departing for Saudi Arabia)

Location: Apartment Window, overlooking a sleepless New York.
Time: 2:43 a.m.
Mood: Shattered soul. A heart trying to find Allah in pieces.

Verses from the Qur'an That Echoed in His Soul

Zaid opened the Qur'an that had long been left untouched on his shelf.

As his tears dripped on the pages, his eyes stopped on verses he had never noticed before or perhaps never needed before.

1. Surah Ar-Ra'd – 13:28

أَلَا بِذِكْرِ اللَّهِ تَطْمَئِنُّ الْقُلُوبُ

"Verily, in the remembrance of Allah do hearts find rest."

2. Surah Al-Baqarah – 2:216

وَعَسَىٰ أَن تَكْرَهُوا شَيْئًا وَهُوَ خَيْرٌ لَكُمْ

"And perhaps you hate a thing while it is good for you."

3. Surah Al-Baqarah – 2:186

وَإِذَا سَأَلَكَ عِبَادِي عَنِّي فَإِنِّي قَرِيبٌ

"And when my servants ask you concerning me – indeed, I am near."

He closed the Qur'an.
And opened his diary one last time this time not for Hayat, but **for himself.**

Bleeding Ink, Burning Soul

"Tere bina jeene ki koshish toh ki,
Par har dua mein tera zikr aa gaya."
    "Main woh safar tha jise koi manzil na mili,
Tu woh dua thi jo qubool hoke bhi rukhsat ho gayi."
    "Log kehte hain waqt badal deta hai sab kuch,
Par waqt ne toh mujhe khud se hi ajnabee bana diya."
    "Hayat chali gayi, lekin mohabbat ki mitti mein ab bhi uski khushboo hai,
Har saans mein ek nida hai 'Tu khuda se mil, mujhse nahi.'"
    "Main be-rooh ho chuka hoon, lekin sajde zinda rakhte hain,
Ek woh hai jo chhod gayi, ek woh hai jo har waqt paas hai"
Mera Rab...

Zaid's Reflections before Leaving

"I came to New York to build a future... but Allah brought me here to break my ego."
"I lost Hayat not because she was mine and slipped away, but because she never was."
"And perhaps... I was never supposed to marry her, but to

feel this heartbreak so I could kneel for the first time not to a woman, but to my Lord."

✈? *Final Lines in His Diary As He Boarded the Flight*

"Nafrat se nahi, duaon se jaa raha hoon,
Uske naseeb mein sukoon ho, bas yahi chahta hoon.
    Main uska na ban saka, yeh meri kismet thi
Par main Allah ka bann jaaun, yeh meri ibadat hai."

دل کے ورق پر آخری تحریر یہ چھوڑ آیا ہوں

خود کو گنوا کر، صرف تجھے پانے کی تقدیر چھوڑ آیا ہوں

جس نے ہنسی چھین لی تھی، آنکھوں سے خواب چرا لیے تھے

اُس "حیات" کے قدموں میں، میں اپنے سانسوں کی زنجیر چھوڑ آیا ہوں

نہ کوئی شکوہ، نہ الزام تیرے فیصلے پر

پر دیکھنا، دعا میں بھی تیرا نام چھوڑ آیا ہوں

خون سے لکھی ہے یہ ڈائری، ہر صفحہ صدا ہے

تو نے نہ سنا، پر میں تیرا ہر درد دل سے سہیل آیا ہوں

راتوں کو روتے ہوئے بس یہی صدا کی

یا رب! جسے چاہا وہ ہی نصیب سے دور آیا ہوں

کبھی میرے سجدوں کا جواب دے دے مولا

کیوں ہر عشق کے بعد صرف "صبر" آیا ہوں

یہ عشق نہیں تھا، سزا تھی کسی گناہ کی

جسے سمجھا تھا جنت، وہی میرا دوزخ بنا آیا ہوں

حیات تو نصیب نہ ہوئی، پر ایک وعدہ تو لیے جا

تو خوش رہنا، میں خود کو درد کی زنجیر بنا آیا ہوں

*Dil ke varaq par aakhiri tahreer ye chhod aaya hoon
Khud ko gawaakar, sirf tujhe paane ki taqdeer chhod aaya hoon.*

Jisne hansi cheen li thi, aankhon se khwaab chura liye the,
Us 'Hayat' ke kadmon mein, main apni saanson ki zanjeer
chhod aaya hoon.

Na koi shikwa, na ilzaam tere faisle par,
Par dekhna, dua mein bhi tera naam chhod aaya hoon.
Khoon se likhi hai ye diary, har panna sada hai,
Tune na suna, par main tera har dard dil se jheel aaya hoon.

Raato ko rote hue bas yahi sada ki,
Ya Rab! Jise chaha wahi naseeb se door aaya hoon.
Kabhi mere sajdon ka jawab de de Maula,
Kyun har ishq ke baad sirf 'sabr' aaya hoon.

Ye ishq nahi tha, saza thi kisi gunaah ki,
Jise samjha tha jannat, wahi mera dozakh bana aaya hoon.
Hayat to naseeb na hui, par ek wada to le ja,
Tu khush rehna, main khud ko dard ki zanjeer bana aaya
hoon.

दलिकवेरकपरआखरितहरीरयेछोड़आयाहूँ

खुदकोगवाँकर, सरि्फतुझेपानेकीतकदीरछोड़आयाहूँ

जसिनेहँसीछीनलीथी, आँखोंसेख्वाबचुरालिएथे,

उस 'हयात' केकदमोंमें, मैंअपनीसाँसोंकीजंज़ीरछोड़आयाहूँ

नाकोईशकिवा, नाइल्ज़ामतेरेफैसलेपर,

परदेखना, दुआमेंभीतेरानामछोड़आयाहूँ

खूनसेलखिीहैयेडायरी, हरपन्नासदाहै,

तूनेनसुना, परमैंतेराहरदर्ददिलिसेझेलआयाहूँ

रातोंकोरोतेहुएबसयहीसदाकी,

यारब! जिसेचाहावहीनसीबसेदूरआयाहूँ

कभीमेरेसज्दोंकाजवाबददेमौला,

क्योंहरइश्कक़ेबादसरि्फ 'सब्र' आयाहूँ

येइश्कनहींथा, सजाथीकिसीगुनाहकी,

जिसेसमझाथाजन्नत, वहीमेरादोज़ख़बनाआयाहूँ

हयातततोनसीबनहुई, परएकवादातोलेजा,

तूखुशरहना, मैंखुदकोदर्दकीज़ंज़ीरबनाआयाहूँ

CHAPTER ELEVEN

The Journey to Redemption

Zaid travels to Saudi Arabia, seeking spiritual refuge and a chance to reclaim lost hope.
The bright lights of New York faded behind him not just as a city, but as a symbol of what he lost. With every mile away from Hayat, Zaid wasn't just distancing himself from a person. He was walking toward something far more eternal **toward Allah.**

He stepped off the plane in **Makkah**, his heart pounding not with fear, but with the broken rhythm of a soul longing for peace.

"أَلاَ بِذِكْرِ اللَّهِ تَطْمَئِنُّ الْقُلُوبُ"

"Verily, in the remembrance of Allah do hearts find rest."
Surah Ar-Ra'd, 13:28

For the first time in years, Zaid wasn't looking for someone's hand to hold he was looking for Allah's forgiveness, His mercy, His acceptance.

Nights in Makkah: Silent Conversations with Allah

In the stillness of the Haram, beneath the black velvet of the Kaaba, he cried like a child.
Not because he was weak.
But because **he was finally free to be weak in front of the One who never abandoned him.**

"وَإِذَا سَأَلَكَ عِبَادِي عَنِّي فَإِنِّي قَرِيبٌ"

"And when My servants ask you concerning Me, indeed I am near."
Surah Al-Baqarah, 2:186

His sajda was no longer just a ritual. It was the only place he truly breathed.
He wept for his past, for Falak's unhealed pain, for Hayat's distance, and for the version of himself that he had lost.

Zaid's Diary Entry in New York (Written Before Leaving)

"Mera ishq sirf mohabbat nahi tha, woh ek sajda tha...
Jis mein maine apne nafs ko jala kar, tujhe paane ki dua ki thi."

"Main haar gaya apne jazbaaton se, lekin jeet gaya us Rabb se,
Jis ne mujhe tere gham mein khud se milwa diya."

"Ab duaon mein naam tera nahi, lekin har dua tere liye hai."

In the Silence of Madinah

Later, in Madinah, at the resting place of the Prophet Muhammad ﷺ, Zaid sat in reflection.
He felt no need for worldly love anymore.
He wanted to become someone **Allah would love.**

"إِنَّ اللَّهَ يُحِبُّ التَّوَّابِينَ وَيُحِبُّ الْمُتَطَهِّرِينَ"

"Indeed, Allah loves those who repent and purify themselves."
Surah Al-Baqarah, 2:222

The wind in Makkah was still, yet it stirred something deep within him. Days passed with Zaid roaming between prayers and tears, but one night under the silence of stars he finally **slept without pain.**

The Dream: A Glimpse of Innocence

In his dream, he was no longer Zaid of New York...
He was Zaid, the young boy in **a small madrasa in Kashmir,** reciting verses with a soft voice and glowing eyes.
He saw **his Ustaad (teacher)** smiling gently, saying:

"Beta, duniya dhoka hai. Har chehra, har rishta sirf ek imtihaan hai.
Asli rishta sirf ek hai woh tere Rabb se hai."

He saw himself reciting from the Qur'an, sitting on a straw mat, with dust in the air and light on his heart.
He felt peace, the kind he hadn't known for years.

Then the dream turned.

He saw himself **hurting the hearts** of women who once loved him girls who had prayed for him, cried for him, and were left with silence.
And then he saw **Falak** again.

In a bridal dress, standing alone in the rain, whispering:

"Zaid, may Allah make you taste the pain you gave others... so you finally understand."

He woke up, **sweating,** breathe shallow. But this time...
Not in restlessness **in realization.**

The Tawbah (Repentance)

Zaid stepped out barefoot, tears washing his cheeks, and made his way to the **Kaaba** in the early hours before Fajr.

There, standing before the House of Allah, he broke down:

"Ya Allah... main gunehgaar hoon.
Har dil ko toda, har rishtay ko khilaaf-e-sunnat chalaaya...
Magar tu hai Ghafur-ur-Raheem.
Mujhe maaf kar de, ya Allah..."

He raised his trembling hands and cried like a child **not out of loss, but longing.**

"قُلْ يَا عِبَادِيَ ٱلَّذِينَ أَسْرَفُوا عَلَىٰ؟ أَنفُسِهِمْ لَا تَقْنَطُوا مِن رَّحْمَةِ ٱللَّهِ"

"Say, O My servants who have transgressed against themselves, do not despair of the mercy of Allah."
Surah Az-Zumar, 39:53

A New Routine, a New Soul

From that day, Zaid created a new life for himself:
Tahajjud became his oxygen.
He spent mornings cleaning the mosque quietly, unseen.
He helped lost Hajj pilgrims find their way.
He read Qur'an not for reward, but for healing.

The boy who once chased the world now **chased forgiveness.**
The man who once broke hearts now **mended his own.**

"Main aashiq tha logon ka,
Ab sirf Rabb ka faqeer ban gaya hoon."

He stopped writing about heartbreaks and started writing **duas** in his journal.

The Final Realization

Nothing is permanent in this world—not beauty, not people, not even pain.
Only Allah remains.

"كُلُّ مَنْ عَلَيْهَا فَانٍ ۝ وَيَبْقَىٰ وَجْهُ رَبِّكَ ذُو الْجَلَالِ وَالْإِكْرَامِ"

"Everything upon the earth will perish, and there will remain the Face of your Lord, Owner of Majesty and Honor."

Surah Ar-Rahman, 55:26-27

Zaid now walked the alleys of Makkah not as a sinner in pain, but as **a soul in peace**.

Hayat was no longer a wound she was a chapter.

Falak was no longer a curse she was a mirror.

And Allah?

Allah was home.

CHAPTER TWELVE

Sajood The Final Prayer

The sun over Makkah had just begun to dip behind the horizon, and the Kaaba glowed softly under the golden veil of dusk. Zaid sat near the white marbled boundary, his eyes scanning the pilgrim's men and women crying, whispering, and praying.

He watched as one old **Haji** sobbed uncontrollably before the Kaaba, his hands trembling, his face drowned in tears, whispering:

"Ya Allah... mere gunah maaf kar de. Main bas tera banda hoon."

O Allah, forgive my sins. I am only your servant.

Something shattered inside Zaid.

The Realization of a Mislaid Dream

That night, as he lay beneath the open sky, he wept bitterly, remembering the dream of his **childhood** to become a **momin**, a righteous servant of Allah. He recalled how, as a boy, he would mimic the imam's recitation and cry out:

"Main Allah ka banda banna chahta hoon."

I want to be a servant of Allah.

But now, **those dreams were mislaid**... scattered like ashes in the wind of his worldly mistakes.

"Mujhse meri rooh bhi sharminda hai,
Woh bacha kahaan chala gaya jo momin banna chahta tha..."

He cursed his past, the love games, the betrayals, and the false pride.

Life is short, he now knew. But the **life after** that's what truly matters.

The Final Sajood

That day, he performed wudhu with trembling hands, and walked again toward the Kaaba.

His **bag lay beside him**, inside it **his diary**.

The pages soaked with tears, ink, and even blood some parts written in heartbreak, others in healing.

The last page was left blank.

He stood for **two rakaats**, and then went down for **sajood**.

"Subhana Rabbiyal A'la..."
Glory be to my Lord, the Most High...

In that sajood, he whispered not his pain but his surrender.

"Ya Allah, main haar gaya hoon.
Ab jo bacha hai, woh sirf tera hai.
Mera dil, meri rooh, mera wajood...
Tu le le, mujhe maaf kar de."

One sajood... then another.

With **every prostration**, Zaid felt the **chains of his sins breaking**.

He felt closer to Allah than he had ever felt to any human being.

And then... came **the last sajood.**
His forehead pressed on the marble floor.
Tears soaked the ground.
A **stillness** took over.
Zaid did not rise again.

The Diary and the Reward

A pilgrim sitting nearby saw him motionless.
He went closer and found Zaid... **lifeless, peaceful, and smiling.**
Beside him, the bag.
Inside: a diary with a note in trembling handwriting:
"Main zindagi haar gaya hoon,
Magar sajood mein jeet gaya hoon."
I lost in life, but in prostration, I found victory.
That Haji handed the diary to the **Imam of Masjid al-Haram.**
The Imam read the pages filled with sins, regrets, tears, repentance, and... love for Allah.
The Imam raised his hand and said:
"Alhamdulillah... Allah ne is bande ko baksh diya hai. Woh akhir mein lot aaya...
Aur Jannatul Baqi uska intezaar kar raha hai."
Praise be to Allah, this servant has been forgiven.
He returned in the end... and Jannatul Baqi awaits him.

Qur'anic Echo

"إنَّ ٱللّٰهَ يُحِبُّ ٱلتَّوَّٰبِينَ وَيُحِبُّ ٱلْمُتَطَهِّرِينَ"
"Indeed, Allah loves those who repent and those who purify themselves."

Surah Al-Baqarah, 2:222

"وَمَن يَغْفِرُ ⬚لذُّنُوبَ إلاَّ ⬚ للهُ"

"And who forgives sins except Allah?"

Surah Aal-e-Imran, 3:135

Zaid's body was bathed and wrapped in the **white cloth of Ihram.**

He was buried not in glamour, but in **grace,** under the soil of **Jannatul Baqi** where the Prophet's companions lie.

His final sajood became his gate to **eternal peace.**

His mislaid dreams were no longer wasted.

They were fulfilled.

In the most beautiful way possible.

"Ya Allah, mujhe aisi maut dena

Jo sajood mein ho,

Tere karam ke saaye mein ho,

Aur mere sab gunah muaf ho jaayein."

Author's Note

Mislaid Dreams was born from moments of deep reflection, countless silent prayers, and a longing to give voice to the unspoken struggles many carry within. Through Zaid's journey, I have tried to capture not just a story, but a shared human experience one that speaks of regret, redemption, faith, and the extraordinary strength it takes to begin again.

This book is not about perfection, but about returning to oneself, to purpose, and most importantly, to **Allah**. It is my humble attempt to remind readers that even in their most fragile state, they are never truly alone.

Thank you for walking this path with me.

Irfan Nazir Wani
Author

Closing Reflection

We all carry dreams some fulfilled, some forgotten, and some we gently lay aside, believing they were never meant to be. But in every mislaid dream lies a lesson, a memory, and sometimes, a path back to faith.

If this book has touched your heart, I ask you to do one thing: pause, reflect, and offer a quiet sujood of gratitude for all that was, all that is, and all that is yet to come.

Because no dream entrusted to Allah is ever truly lost.